Voices

Sheffield Flood

b ... the General Cemetery

Sue Turner

Sue Turner

Sheffield General Cemetery Trust

Acknowledgements

The Sheffield General Cemetery Trust gratefully acknowledges the Sheffield City Archive and Local Studies Library for their ongoing support.

A special thank you to Karen Lightowler for so generously allowing access to her resources, sharing her knowledge and use of her research. Thank you to Malcolm Nunn from Bradfield Archives and to all the staff at the Trust who contributed their time and expertise particularly Shirley Baxter, Helen Brown, Ruth Hoffman, Jean Lees, Andrew Littlewood, Marcin Nikoniuk, Phil Parnham and Cathy Spence.

Sheffield General Cemetery Trust

Cover illustration: Photograph taken near to the Turner Wheel at Malin Bridge by Laurence Peacock
Printed by Mensa Printers, 323 Abbeydale Road, Sheffield, S7 1FS
ISBN: 978-1-7390808-9-1

Published by Sheffield General Cemetery Trust 2024

It seemed as if the bowels of the earth were being torn up, or as if some … monster were rushing down the valley, lashing the hill sides with his scaly folds, crunching up buildings between his jaws, and filling all the air with his wrathful hiss…

… trees snapped like pistols, mills and houses stood and staggered for a moment, and then disappeared in the boiling torrent.

Eyewitness account of John Ibbotson of Bradfield, 1864

Drowned Voices is an account of the lives and deaths of people buried in Sheffield General Cemetery who lost their lives in the Sheffield Flood of 1864. It includes details of how they met their fate and the consequences for their immediate family.

Contents

Introduction

The mid-19th century was a time of great change in Sheffield as many people moved into the town from rural areas in search of work. The population of the town increased from 45,758 in 1801 to 135,310 by 1851 and, while the industrial revolution brought wealth to the factory owners and jobs for the poor, the growth in population put pressure on the services provided such as housing, sanitation and healthcare. Life expectancy was short due not only to poor sanitation, but cramped living conditions, contaminated water, poor diet and hazardous working environments.

The burial grounds in the centre of the town were literally full to overflowing and several epidemics swept the town in the early 1830s. In 1834 a group of Nonconformists formed the Sheffield General Cemetery Company to remedy the situation. Nine acres of steeply sloping, north facing land was bought in the lower part of the Porter Valley and in 1836 the Cemetery opened, as described in William White's 1837 *Gazetteer and General Directory of Sheffield*, "for the perambulations of the living and a safe depository for the dead".

A good clean water supply was vital to the town, needed by the residents for drinking and sanitation and for turning the waterwheels that drove the mills and machinery that the town's reputation was built on. As the population increased in parallel with the growth in industry the Sheffield authorities needed to increase the town's water supply. By the early 1850s the Sheffield Waterworks Company had plans for the building of three new reservoirs on the Bradfield Moors. One of the dams, Dale Dyke, had problems early in its construction and plans had to be revised, the site of the embankment being moved further upstream. Work was then delayed still further by flooding but by March 1864 the reservoir was nearing completion and was almost full.

Friday 11 March was wet and stormy, and the resident engineer, John Gunson, visited the site in the afternoon to see how it was coping with the weather conditions. Gunson returned to Sheffield confident that all was well, and that the reservoir could deal with the atrocious weather to which it was being exposed. Later that day, back at the dam a crack in the embankment was found and a message sent down the valley to get the engineer to return. On inspecting the embankment, Gunson ordered that part of the weir should be blown away with gunpowder to lower the level of the water. With the gunpowder failing to blow, he decided to increase the flow of water through the outlet pipes but as he did so, a 30ft length of the embankment broke away and water began to pour through. Gunson and his workers ran for their lives as the flow developed into a raging deluge and more of the embankment gave way. An explosion was heard as the gunpowder finally blew and the contents of the reservoir crashed through the embankment. An estimated 650 million gallons of water thundered down the valley leaving a gap in the embankment 110 yards long and about 70 feet deep.

> The gunpowder under the weir exploded, and at once the embankment fully stretched its monstrous jaws. The flood was at liberty, and, with the noise of thunder, the swiftness of lightning, and the force of Niagara, it leapt into the valley below.
>
> Hunter's Hallamshire

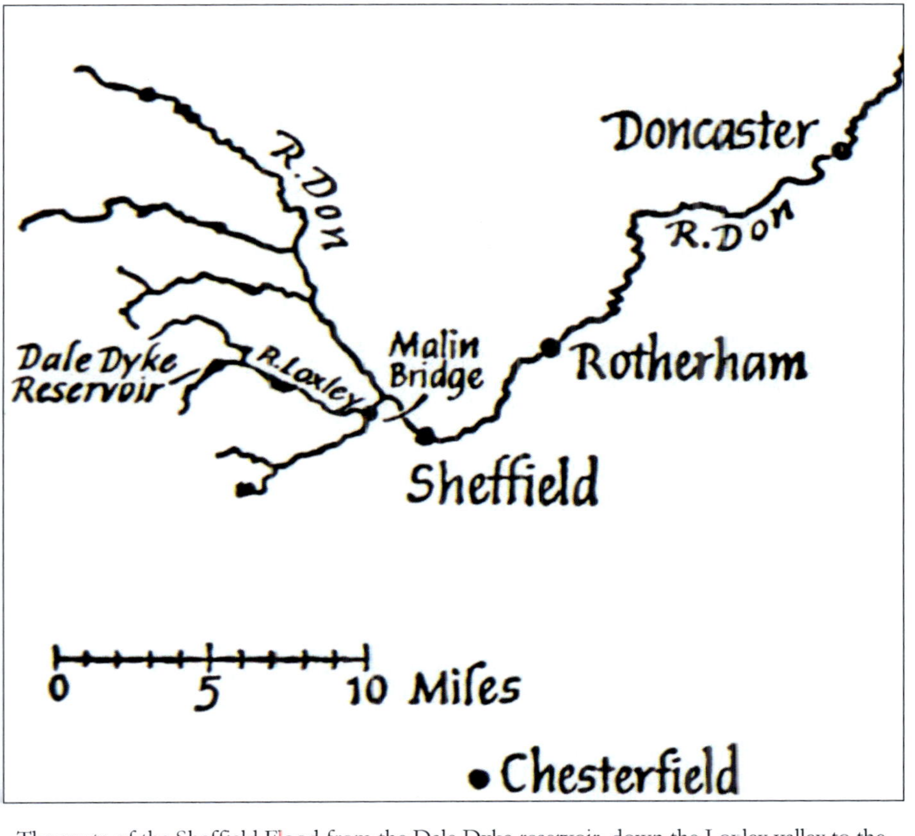

The route of the Sheffield Flood from the Dale Dyke reservoir, down the Loxley valley to the River Don, through Sheffield town centre and on to Rotherham and Doncaster.

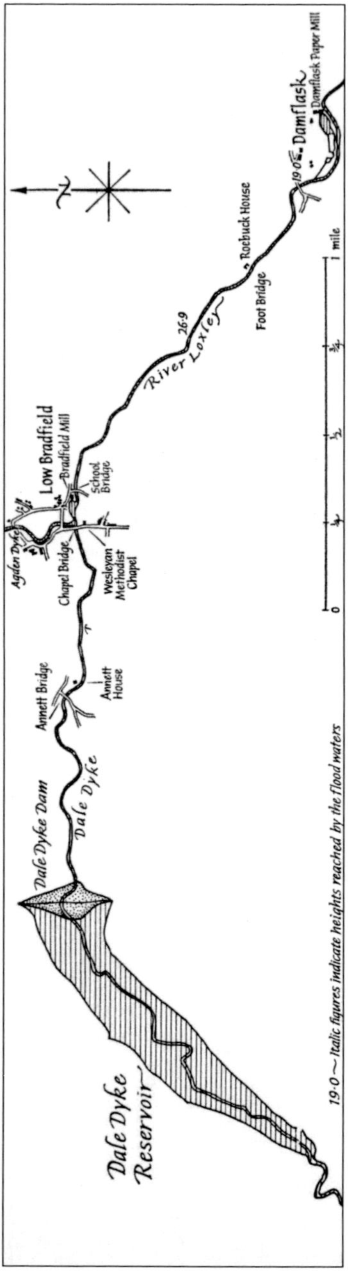

Dale Dyke Reservoir
Dale Dyke Dam
Dale Dyke
Annett Bridge
Annett House
Chapel Bridge
Wesleyan Methodist Chapel
Agden Dyke
Low Bradfield
Bradfield Mill
School Bridge
River Loxley
26·9
Foot Bridge
Roebuck House
19·0
Damflask
Damflask Paper Mill
N
0
¼
½
¾
1 mile
19·0 ~ Italic figures indicate heights reached by the flood waters

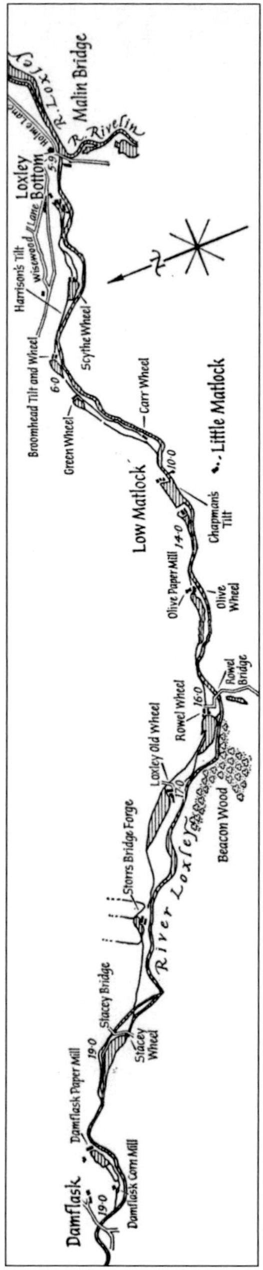

Damflask
19·0
Damflask Corn Mill
Damflask Paper Mill
19·0
Stacey Bridge
Stacey Wheel
River Loxley
Storrs Bridge Forge
Beacon Wood
Loxley Old Wheel
17·0
Rowel Wheel
16·0
Rowel Bridge
Olive Paper Mill
Olive Wheel
14·0
Low Matlock
Chapman's Tilt
10·0
Little Matlock
Green Wheel
Carr Wheel
Broomhead Tilt and Wheel
6·0
Scythe Wheel
Harrison's Tilt
Wisewood Lane
Loxley Bottom
5·9
Holme Lane
R. Loxley
R. Rivelin
Malin Bridge
N

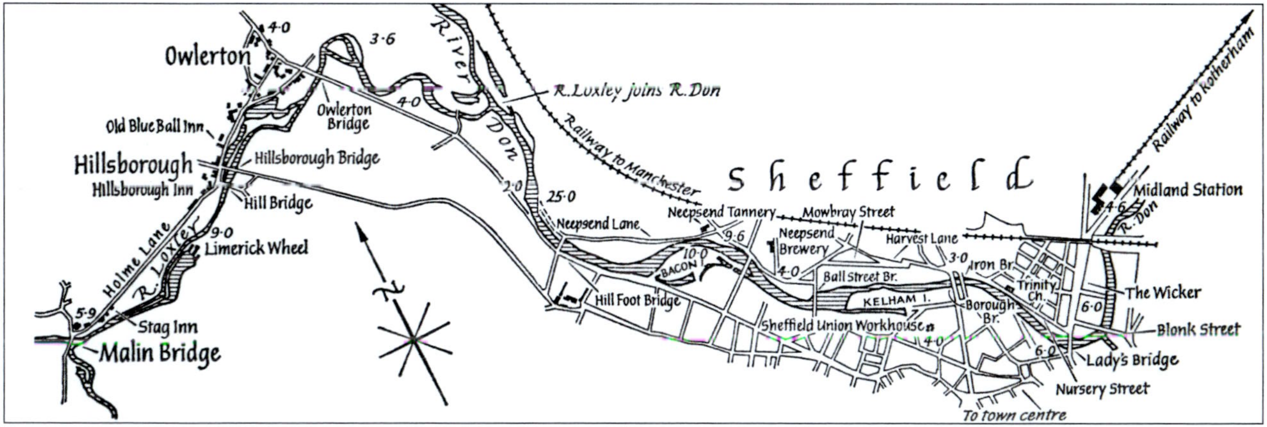

The route of the Sheffield Flood from (top) the Dale Dyke reservoir to Dam Flask, (middle) Dam Flask to Malin Bridge and (bottom) Malin Bridge to Sheffield town centre.

The Deluge

The deluge forced its way down towards Low Bradfield destroying everything in its path. Trees were ripped from the ground; buildings were washed away, and bridges destroyed. Many of the inhabitants of Low Bradfield, either being involved in the building of the Dam or knowing people who were, had received warnings that all was not well and had moved to higher ground. Thus, there was less loss of life in the village compared to others downstream, but nothing could be done to save homes and belongings.

The wall of water and the debris it carried raced on towards Dam Flask where homes, the bridge and an inn were destroyed. Lives were lost and survivors left devastated. Along the course of the river a corn mill, wire mills and a grinding wheel were all swept away, the force relentless and no building left unscathed. The brick kiln at Storrs Bridge was destroyed and the scene at the Bridge after the Flood was described by Samuel Harrison in *A Complete History of the Great Flood of Sheffield on March 11 and 12, 1864*, as

> one of great desolation and ruin. Huge stones were scattered about, and trees, torn up by their roots, lay in and near the stream, some embedded in the mud, and others covered with hay and rubbish of every description.

Loxley Old Wheel with its surrounding cottages and outbuildings took the full force of the water as did Thomas Wragg's Brickworks where over 19,000 bricks were washed away along with the building. Continuing down the valley several grinding wheels were destroyed at Rowell Bridge plus a corn mill, The Bridge Inn public house, adjoining cottages and Rowell Bridge itself. More lives lost; another community shattered.

Flood damage at Rowell Bridge Wheel
looking towards The Bridge Inn, photographer Laurence Peacock

Further down the valley it was fortunate that nobody was working at the Olive Grinding Wheel which was destroyed or the Olive Paper Mill which was severely damaged. Relentlessly onward raged the torrent claiming homes, gardens, orchards and grinding wheels. The tilt hammers and rolling mills of Little Matlock with the adjacent cottages all caught the full force of the Flood; more lives were lost, and futures ruined. Here the valley opened out allowing the water to fan out and deposit rocks, debris and bodies in the mud before being channelled again into a narrower valley as it approached Malin Bridge. There were few homes along this stretch of river but many wheels, some of which were totally washed away. The raging torrent thundered on destroying a succession of mills, tilts and forges and leaving a landscape of devastation with wheels and heavy machinery sticking up out of the mud. As the water reached the end of the Loxley Valley the lives of 18 people had been lost and many homes demolished.

William Longley and his wife Mary Ellen, née Winks, lived near Malin Bridge with their two children Jane Ann and Mary Elizabeth. William Longley worked at Damflask Wire Mill where it was normal to work all night. He was there with three other workers when the Flood hit, part of the mill was swept away and all four were drowned. The other members of his family died at home. An insurance claim was initially made for £300 by William's father, also William Longley, in respect of the loss of his son's life. This was withdrawn and a claim made in respect of the damage to his son's personal property. The claim included a woollen flock bed, child's bed, cradle, pillows, a mattress, sheets and blankets plus the family's clothes. Tables, chairs, pictures, crockery, candlesticks and an "alarum clock" were also in the claim as was "Loss of Time and Expenses in coming to Sheffield searching for the Body". William Longley, senior, a coachmaker who lived in Saddleworth, claimed a total of £20 5s and was awarded £22 7s. This was one of very few claims that received more than the amount requested.

The body of William Longley was recovered over five weeks after his death. The bodies of Mary Ellen Longley aged 26, and the two children, Jane Ann, aged 4, and Mary, aged 18 months were never identified.

William Longley, aged 30, was buried on 20 April in the Anglican area of the Cemetery in plot X2 140, a public grave with no memorial stone.

Remains of F. Shaw and Co., wire drawers, Damflask Wire Mill, River Loxley looking downstream, photographer Laurence Peacock

Malin Bridge

The village of Malin Bridge, about five miles from Dale Dyke, was a busy and self-sufficient community with, as well as the local metal industries and agriculture, several shops which served the residents. There were butchers, grocers, drapers, tailors, cobblers and general stores, four pubs and at least one tradesperson offered plumbing, glazing and painting. Malin Bridge took the full force of the Flood water, with 102 residents losing their lives including five entire families. Grinding wheels, rolling mills, corn mills, tilt hammers, snuff mills and other water-related industries and workings plus homes, shops and inns were all inundated by the Flood. An imposing farmhouse stood near the junction of the rivers Loxley and Rivelin and its ten occupants all lost their lives.

Near to the farm was a row of three cottages and all were demolished by the power of the water. In one was living James Bagshaw, an Anvil Maker, and his wife Mary, aged 45 and 58 respectively. Both lost their lives that night. Mary Bagshaw was buried on 15 March in the graveyard at Wadsley Church.

James Bagshaw, aged 45, was buried in the Anglican area of the Cemetery on 5 May in plot G3 30, a public grave with no memorial stone.

RUINS OF WISEWOOD WORKS.

WHERE THE BRIDGE CROSSED THE RIVER AT MALIN BRIDGE.

Below the confluence of the rivers Loxley and Rivelin and on the left bank stood a row of twelve cottages known as Bower's Buildings. They bore the brunt of the full force of the river and, not being of the best quality construction, they vanished into the raging torrent along with their occupants, disappearing as though they had never existed. In one of the cottages lived George Barrott, aged 24, a shoemaker, his wife Emma, aged 21, a 22-month-old child, William, and a 50-year-old lodger named Ann Pearson. George Barrott, born at Malin Bridge, had married Emma in the summer of 1860 and initially the couple lived in the Old Barrack Buildings on Penistone Road. Their son William was born in 1862. The bodies of George and his son William were never found. The body of Emma Barrott was found two weeks later and interred at Wardsend Cemetery on 28 March. No claim was made for either the Barrott family or Ann Pearson.

Ann Pearson, aged 50, was buried in the Anglican area of the Cemetery on 15 March in plot M3 21, a public grave with no memorial stone.

Down from Malin Bridge was the Limerick Wheel, a crinoline wire manufactory occupied by Messrs Johnson and Barker. The building sustained considerable damage with the end of the solid stone building being driven in, machinery damaged or destroyed, the boiler house swept away, and two large boilers left exposed and stripped of their coverings. For a considerable distance downstream, the riverbanks were strewn with rolls of crinoline wire, pieces of machinery and heavy tools used by the workmen. The damage to the works was estimated at £10,000.

Coloured engraving of the scene following the Sheffield Flood: Barker and Johnson's crinoline factory, Malin Bridge

Some months previously there had been men working at the Wheel day and night but on the night of the Flood there was only one man present. That was William Bethell from Masborough and he was on his way home when he met a carter going to the works with a load of steel. The carter told Bethell he must go back to the works to soften the steel that night or it would keep the men out of work for several days.

Bethell then went back and was preparing the steel for the subsequent processes of manufacture when he was overtaken

> by the flood. His body was not found till some weeks afterwards when it was discovered in the works beneath a heap of rubbish. It was frightfully disfigured and scalded. It is believed that the works were destroyed more by an explosion than by the force of the water. In one furnace there were thirty hundredweights of steel, and a large quantity in four other furnaces, all red-hot, and when the water came in steam would be at once generated to an extent that would cause a fearful explosion, the report of which was actually heard by persons who lived near.
>
> *A Complete History of the Great Flood of Sheffield,* Samuel Harrison, 1864

On the loss of her husband, Elizabeth Bethell, like many other Flood victims' widows, was left with no income and herself and three young children to feed. According to the *Sheffield Daily Telegraph* of 18 April 1864 William Bethell's "very much decomposed" body was found in the ruins of the Limerick Wheel on 16 April and his wife informed.

William Bethell, aged 38, was buried in the Anglican area of the Cemetery on 17 April in plot X2 161, a public grave with no memorial stone. On 18 April, William Bethell's body was removed at the request of his wife to Rotherham Moorgate Cemetery.

Elizabeth Bethell as the wife of William Bethell made a claim totalling £2650 for herself and her three children. Her claim was assessed in February 1865 and Mr Motteram, a barrister of Birmingham appeared in support of the claim. The Commissioners awarded Elizabeth Bethell £1,000, (the highest grant given) £550 for herself, £125 for Elizabeth Caroline Bethell, aged 5, £150 for Frances Georgina Bethell aged 3 and £175 for Annie Gertrude Bethell, aged 18 months.

In June 1868 Elizabeth Bethell, then aged 33, married 27-year-old bachelor Edwin Edwards, an accountant, at Manchester Cathedral. Elizabeth Edwards was widowed a second time in 1887 and died in Manchester in 1905 aged 75.

Just below the Limerick Wheel in an area known as Hill Bridge, was a community of 20 small houses and the Freemasons Arms public house. Despite being a strong, well-built structure, Hill Bridge was destroyed and ten people lost their lives in the area including the landlord of the Freemasons Arms, William Pickering, aged 34, his wife Charlotte Ann, aged 23, his sister Elizabeth aged 23 and an unnamed lodger. At the Freemasons Arms that night was William Pickering's 8-year-old niece, Mary Ann. Mary Ann Pickering survived the Flood, sleeping in the top storey of the house, above the water line.

> When the neighbours went to the house on the morning after the flood, they found that nearly everything had been swept away, but on going to the upper chamber they were astonished to find the little girl in bed and fast asleep. They awoke her, and took her to a place of safety. The house was swept away except a little corner on which the girl's bed stood. Upon being questioned she said – "I heard a noise in the middle of the night. I thought the gas was blowing up down stairs. I heard my uncle go down stairs, and thought he was going to see if the gas had blown up. I then heard my aunt go down, and call out for help. Her sister went to her, and I then heard them both cry out for help. I heard nothing more, and went to sleep soon afterwards."
>
> *A Complete History of the Great Flood of Sheffield,* Samuel Harrison, 1864

The remains of Hill Bridge and the Freemasons Arms, photographer Laurence Peacock The houses on the right in the photograph were white-washed and the height of the flood can be seen on the tidemark left on them. This proved of great interest to sightseers who came to view the devastation and the high watermark remained on the houses for years after the Flood.

The body of William Pickering was never found but those of his wife and sister were buried in a family plot in the Cemetery. Already buried in the plot were William Pickering's uncle John Pickering, a manager at a steel works, and his cousin John Pickering, a grinder.

Charlotte Ann Pickering and Elizabeth Pickering, both aged 23, were buried on 15 March in the Nonconformist area of the Cemetery in plot G 120. The body of William Pickering was never identified but he was memorialised on plot G 120.

Elizabeth and William Pickering's mother Mary, aged 66 years, of Matlock Bath, made two claims as Administrator of their estate and effects. The effects of Elizabeth were a large quantity of clothing as she was about to be married which was assessed at £15. The claim for the effects of William suggests a well-furnished dwelling with a "best sitting room" containing a mahogany dining table, a hair seated sofa with six chairs, a carpet, an eight day clock and books in a bookcase which included "some good works". Also in the home were two silver watches, silver teaspoons and sugar tongs, china cups and saucers and boxes of cigars. The bar of the Freemasons Arms was well stocked with 280 gallons of beer, 54 gallons of ale, six gallons of vinegar, four gallons of cordial and there was £25 cash in the building. The claim included the expense of the 13 working days it took to clean the premises. Mary Pickering received £150.

Whilst eight-year-old Mary Ann Pickering survived the Flood she was impacted psychologically. Her father Alfred Pickering a saw grinder, filed a claim on her behalf. He claimed £20 as "the memory of the said Mary Ann Pickering is much impaired she is in a depressed state of mind raves about the water requires much time and attention and has been compelled to be sent from home". The claim was assessed and £10 awarded.

Mary Ann Pickering married William Henry Champion, a table knife cutler, in 1876 and had two children, Henry born in 1879 and Mary born in 1883.

Mary Ann Champion died in 1932, aged 75, and was buried with her parents and husband in the Nonconformist area of the Cemetery in plot N 145.

In a house close to the Freemasons Arms lived George Snape, a 41-year-old labourer and shop keeper, and his wife Mary, aged 45. George Snape was unwell at the time of the Flood, suffering from arthritis and was confined to his bed in a room on the ground floor. As the Flood burst into their house, he and his wife were instant victims, drowned in their bed. The *Sheffield and Rotherham Independent* of 14 March 1864 reported that Mary was found nearby and her body taken to the Queen's Hotel, Langsett Road where she was identified before being taken for burial at Wardsend Cemetery. George Snape's body was washed down the river to Neepsend.

George Snape, age 41, was buried in the Anglican area of the Cemetery on 14 March in plot Q2 128, a public grave with no memorial stone.

The administrator of George Snape's estate claimed £46 4s 8d for his effects which included household effects, his wife's clothes and "Goods for Sale in Shop". £20 was awarded. £800 was also claimed for the benefit of George and Mary Snape's three children, William aged 17, Jane aged 15 and George aged 9. £110 was awarded.

The remains of Brick Row, Holme Lane, Hillsborough

On leaving Malin Bridge and nearing Hill Bridge the Flood waters reached Brick Row on Holme Lane, a row of 18 three-storied back-to-back houses which had been built in 1853-54. While seven of the houses were unoccupied, others were very crowded and twelve of the residents lost their lives. Isaac Turner, a saw grinder, and his family lived close by and on the night of the Flood, 2-year-old Herbert Gravenor Marshall, the son of a Sheffield pawnbroker, William Wright Marshall, was staying with them. The four members of the Turner family and Herbert Gravenor Marshall perished in the Flood.

William Wright Marshall had married Clara Linley in Sheffield in 1859 and Herbert Gravenor Marshall was their second son. Born on 20 March 1862 he had been baptized on 17 February 1864, at the same time as his brother Harry Somerville Marshall at Queen Street Independent Chapel. The death of one child must have been devastating but just three months later, Harry Somerville Marshall also died aged just eight months and two weeks. The actual cause on his death certificate was "found dead in bed" but it is believed within the family that his death was caused by being caught up in the Flood. The two boys were buried in the grave bought by their grandfather, Christopher Marshall, on the death of his first wife Jane, in June 1836. Jane Marshall was only the third person to be buried in the Cemetery.

Herbert Gravenor Marshall, aged 2, was buried on 15 March and Harry Sommerville Marshall, aged 8 months, on 12 June in the Nonconformist area of the Cemetery in plot LL 69.

William Wright Marshall claimed £150 for the loss of his son and was awarded £5 and £10 17s 9d for the child's clothing for which he was awarded £9. Evidently the material possessions were valued more highly than the life of a child.

THE RUINS AT HILLSBRO'.

Hillsborough

Hillsborough in 1864 was a small community which had grown around the industry along the River Loxley, with its own shops and public houses. One shop, a general store, was run by John Cowton Appleby and with him that night were his mother Mary Appleby and his niece also called Mary Appleby.

John Cowton Appleby was a widower, his wife Ellen having died the previous year. Although his house was well built of stone, it was partially destroyed and the Applebys swept to their deaths. John Appleby's body was found at Club Mill and his mother's at Jordan Meadows, Rotherham. A claim on his life was made on behalf of his daughter, three-year-old Annie Maria Appleby for £750, £200 being awarded. After the deaths of both her parents Annie Maria Appleby lived with her aunt Eliza Swift on Pomona Steet.

The claim on John Cowton Appleby's estate shows the stock of his grocery shop as well as time spent searching for his body, washing and dressing it and other funeral expenses. £98 7s 4d was claimed, £65 was awarded.

John Appleby's niece Mary was the daughter of his brother Stephen Cowton Appleby and wife Elizabeth. Elizabeth had died shortly after Mary was born in 1851 and by 1864 Stephen Cowton Appleby had remarried and had a young family. His 13-year-old daughter Mary lived with her grandmother and was in the house when the Flood struck.

IN MEMORY OF

John Cowton Appleby,

AGED 36,

Mary, his Mother, 63, & his Niece Mary, 13,

ALL OF HILLSBRO',

Who perished in the Great Flood, occasioned by the bursting of the Bradfield Reservoir, March 12th, 1864, when 258 Lives were lost, and property to the amount of £500,000 destroyed.

The sheet of water covered an area of 78 Acres; depth, 95 feet; dam-head, 400 yards across; and contained 114,000000 cubic feet of water. It was situated 9 miles north west of Sheffield.

In the Ruins of the House the following Recipe was found:—

OILS FOR RHEUMATIC.

1oz. of Oil of Amber.
1oz. of Oil of Spike.
1oz. of Oil of Swallow.
1oz. of Spirit of Sal Ammoniac.
Mix together.

His amiability and virtue commanded respect from all who knew him.

Make sure for your souls who have not been drown'd
Life is uncertain, soon death may be found,
While you live, live well, and strive to be good,
Is our advice who perished in the flood;
Seek virtue, shun vice, have heaven in view,
Serve God, love Christ, and to sin bid adieu.
Amen!

Memorial card for John Cowton Appleby and his family

Mary's body was found at Neepsend and a claim on her life was made by her father Stephen Cowton Appleby for £200. £12 2s was awarded. Stephen Cowton Appleby also made a claim for Mary's clothing, time spent searching for her body, a coffin, burial fees, hearse and mourning coach. £10 15s 6d was claimed and £5 11s 6d was awarded.

Mary Appleby, 63 years old, was the widow of Cowton Appleby by whom she had at least nine children. She was in the home of her son John Cowton Appleby when the Flood struck. A claim on her

Coloured engraving of the scene following the Sheffield Flood: remains of the bridge, Hillsborough

belongings was made by her son Cowton Appleby for £39 13s and £24 was awarded. The claim details show furniture, clothing, framed pictures, several books including a Large Family Bible as well as the expense of searching for her body, washing it and conveying it from Rotherham. It also claimed for a coffin, burial fees, hearse and mourning coach.

Mary Appleby, aged 63, was buried on 15 March in the Anglican area of the Cemetery in plot B3 175 a family plot bought previously by her on the death of her son William in 1858. Her son John Coulton Appleby, aged 32 (according to his burial record), and her granddaughter Mary Appleby, aged 13, were buried in the same plot on 17 March.

As the Flood water raced on, damage was caused to The Shakespeare Inn and the Old Blue Ball Inn near Hillsborough Bridge although both survived while small cottages, stables and an outdoor bowling alley fared less well. It had taken the head of the water about half an hour to reach this point, but it still carried a huge force capable of more death and destruction as it followed the course of the River Loxley.

Owlerton

Through the village of Owlerton more houses were destroyed, mills wrecked and lives lost. Marshall's Paper Mill took the full force of the current and was greatly damaged. The warehouse and drying room were completely carried away and a large hydraulic press, weighing several tons, was torn up from its foundation and washed some distance downstream. In a cottage near to the Paper Mill 54-year-old paper maker, John Turton, and his 72-year-old wife, Susannah, both perished. Their cottage was lifted from its foundations and carried down the river. John Turton's body was found two days later at Neepsend and one day after that, Susannah Turton's body was also found in the same area.

William John Turton, aged 54, and Susannah Turton, aged 72, were buried in the Anglican area of the Cemetery on 15 March in plot Q2 138, a public plot with no memorial stone.

No claim was made for the loss of the lives of the Turtons or their possessions.

The waters raced on, sweeping over the open fields and crashing into the boundary wall of the Hillsborough Barracks with a force capable of demolishing the three-foot-high stone-built wall. There were relatively few deaths at Owlerton considering the extensive damage caused; some of the bodies found there were washed down from communities higher up the valley. Many of the claims made at Owlerton were for "injury to body", mainly from illness and fever as a result of being immersed in the cold and contaminated water. Up to this point, six miles from the Dam, over 150 people had perished and as the water turned towards Sheffield more lives were to be lost and livelihoods destroyed.

More mills along the river were demolished or badly damaged before the waters veered right towards the meadows at the bottom of the hillside below Wardsend Cemetery then headed on towards Hillfoot and Neepsend. The Flood water had lost some of its original impetus by the time it reached the confluence of the Rivers Loxley and Don, but the waters of the River Don, swollen by recent heavy rain, now added to its force.

Mr. HAWKSLEY'S MILL AT OWLERTON.

THE LOW BRIDGE AT OWLERTON.

Neepsend

Neepsend was an extensive, low-lying, heavily populated area on the north side of the River Don and was, after Malin Bridge, the second worst hit area in terms of loss of life. The damage here was appalling with numbers of houses wholly or partially destroyed, and the whole locality flooded. The then Chief Constable, John Jackson's official list of the dead recorded 78 people losing their lives here and many more would die in the coming days and months. Much damage was done both to industrial and domestic premises, bridges were destroyed, and roads left under mud and littered with debris including corpses, both human and animal.

A large area of land at Neepsend was covered by gardens on which were small cottages, some no more than shacks, and many were occupied by families. These flimsy garden hovels stood no chance against the Flood water as it swept through the area destroying the buildings, depositing wreckage and taking lives.

Susannah Kitchen married John Smith Gilyatt in Lincoln in 1833 but the couple do not seem to have stayed together very long, he remaining in Lincolnshire whilst she established a life in Sheffield. **Susannah Gilyatt** was living at Fentonville Gardens before the Flood with her daughter Elizabeth, son-in-law Charles Spencer and five grandchildren under nine years old. Susannah Gilyatt died as the waters came through the area. A claim for £50 for the loss of her life by another daughter Maria Perks was withdrawn. A second claim of £41 18s 6d for the loss of her personal property and funeral expenses was assessed at £12 10s.

Susan Gilyatt was buried in the Anglican area of the Cemetery on 13 March in plot M3 21, a public grave with no memorial stone.

William Coggin, 36 years old, and his 34-year-old wife Elizabeth were away from their Sheffield home on the night of the Flood, attending the funeral of Elizabeth's sister. Their three children, Alfred Coggin, 11 years old, Eliza Coggin, 8 years old and 6-year-old William Coggin had been left at home at Neepsend where a neighbour, Mrs Smith, had promised to keep an eye on them. The family lived in the cellar of their home and here the children were sleeping when the water entered the building, flooding the lower storey and filling the cellar to the ceiling. The children did not stand a chance and were all drowned.

> They were all three found in bed next morning. As though they had never awoken from their slumbers, but had passed quietly away to a sleep more lasting and more profound.
>
> *A Complete History of the Great Flood of Sheffield,* Samuel Harrison, 1864

The children's father William Coggin made a claim of £450 for the loss of life of his three children, £350 for Alfred, £50 for Eliza and £50 for William. The claim was withdrawn with a new one claiming £350 just for the loss of life of Alfred. William Coggin may have been advised to do this as Alfred, at the age of 11 and working as a skinner at 8/- per week, was the only child of material value and this seems to have been the accepted norm in the claims process. William Coggin was awarded £25.

As if this story is not sad enough, William and Elizabeth Coggin had already buried two of their children, James aged 2 and Ada 9 months at Burngreave Cemetery in March 1863. Elizabeth Coggin was pregnant at the time of the Flood, giving birth to Henry Coggin who was baptised on 28 August 1864 at St Jude's Moorfield. They were to bury Jane aged 17 months in June 1867, Henry aged 5 in February 1869 and Mary Ellen aged 10 months in December 1869 all in Burngreave Cemetery, meaning they lost eight children within six years.

Alfred, aged 11, Eliza, aged 8, and William Coggin, aged 6, were buried in the Anglican area of the Cemetery on 14 March in plot G2 126, a public grave with no memorial stone.

John Midwood, a 46-year-old stone mason and his 36-year-old wife Pheobe lived in one of the larger houses on Neepsend Lane with four children, Dawson, named after his mother's maiden name, aged 16, George aged 8, Fanny aged 4 and Joel aged 20, John's son by a previous marriage. The family had retired to bed at the usual time, but Joel Midwood, unable to sleep, heard the noise of water coming nearer and nearer. When he got up to investigate, he found his way downstairs barred by rising water, and in his desperation to get out of the building, he smashed his way through the ceiling and the roof tiles, then climbed onto the roof.

> The flood in the house had raised his father and mother upon their beds almost to the ceiling; and then came a huge baulk of timber down the stream; it struck the house with immense force, and took the gable end with it. His father and mother, amidst the wildest surprise and alarm, came out from this great aperture, floating up on the bed mattress, and the son, knowing their position, watched for them, and, leaning from the roof, upon which he was astride, caught both of them by their hair of their head. The father got upon the roof more readily than the mother, for she had her daughter of five years in her arms, to whom she was clung tenaciously and with true maternal affection. It was a terrible struggle for life, but the son kept his hold, and she reached the roof at last. There the four were, wet and cold, and terrified. But they had not much time for contemplation and sorrowing. Another mass of wood struck the building under them and knocked it down completely, the roof itself floating upon the water. Away they all went rapidly down

> the river; and as they passed the gas works gates, the son noticed a lamp, which had not gone out; it appeared to be only nine or ten inches above the flood. Directly after that he heard his father say, "We're going!" and they sank in a moment – he, his mother, and his young sister. His brothers he never saw again.
>
> *Sheffield Weekly Telegraph,* 13 March 1886

Joel Midwood survived this ordeal by clinging onto accumulated wreckage but not without injuries to his legs, ankles and feet including a wound from a large nail which penetrated his foot. He was taken to the home of his employer, a master builder named George Glentworth, who made him welcome, found him clothes, food and a bed to sleep in. The next day Joel Midwood visited the Workhouse and was able to identify the body of his father which had been found at Rutland Bridge, the body of his mother which had been picked up near Neepsend School and his younger brother. He was not able to find the bodies of either his elder brother or his little sister but did help in the identification of some of the family's neighbours.

Joel Midwood made a claim for £5 8s for the lameness which incapacitated him as he was unable to work for four weeks. In a rare decision by the claims panel, he was awarded £5 18s 6d, more than he had claimed for. In later life he established himself as a builder and was responsible for, amongst other buildings, Almshouses in the Rivelin Valley and the Wycliffe Hall in Channing Street. Joel Midwood died in July 1899, at the age of 54, at 74 Whitehouse Road, having been married three times and having eight children.

His second wife Emma was buried in the General Cemetery in 1886 in the Anglican area in plot H4 22.

The claim for John Midwood's possessions included a four-poster bed, carpets, linen, chairs, tables, clothes and a 22 stone pig! Of the £184 13s 2d claimed, £96 3s was awarded.
The bodies of Dawson and Fanny Midwood were never found, and the burial place of John Midwood has not been traced.

Pheobe Midwood, aged 36, was buried in the Anglican area of the Cemetery on 15 March in plot Q2 136, a public grave with no memorial stone.
George Midwood, aged 8, was buried in the Anglican area of the Cemetery on 15 March in plot T2 4, a public grave with no memorial stone.

> On the bank of the river at Neepsend were several small whitewashed cottages, in one of which lived John Gannon, a labourer, his wife, and six children. Gannon and his family were awoken by the water rising into their bedroom, and seeing the peril in which they were placed they screamed out for help, their shrieks being distinctly heard by the neighbours louder even than the roar of the tempest. The water still rose higher and higher, and, as a last expedient, Gannon got on to the roof of the house, and then lifted up his wife and children. Here they remained for a few minutes, naked, terror-stricken, and piercing the air with their cries for help. The flood continued to increase, till it rose to the top of the house, lifted it up, and carried it away, with all its former inmates, into the seething roaring flood, where they all immediately perished, almost before their last wail of terror had time to ascend from the bosom of the water in which they were instantly engulfed.
>
> *A Complete History of the Great Flood of Sheffield,* Samuel Harrison, 1864

All the members of the Gannon family perished gaining the unwanted distinction of being the family with the highest loss of life in a single family in a single household. The body of Sarah Ann Gannon was not found, and the burial of John junior has not been traced.

The parents John, aged 36, and Sarah Gannon, aged 30, were buried in the Nonconformist area of the Cemetery on 15 March in plot MM 42, a public grave with no memorial stone.
Henry Gannon, aged 11, was buried in the Nonconformist area of the Cemetery on 15 March in plot MM 76, a public grave with no memorial stone.
Peter Gannon, aged 5½, was buried in the Nonconformist area of the Cemetery on 15 March in plot MM 56, a public grave with no memorial stone.
William Gannon, aged 4, was buried in the Nonconformist area of the Cemetery on 15 March in plot MM 46, a public grave with no memorial stone.
Margaret Gannon, aged 4 months, was buried in the Nonconformist area of the Cemetery on 15 March in plot MM 27, a public grave with no memorial stone.

There was no claim for loss of life submitted for the Gannon family.

Thomas Halbert, a dealer in hides and skins, and his wife Catherine, lived in the lower part of the Mills Building on Harvest Lane with their three children, John, five years old, Thomas junior, three years old and Mary Jane, just ten months old. Thomas, Catherine and John Halbert were born in Ireland but had left for a better life in England. On the night of the Flood, Thomas Halbert was woken from his sleep by the noise of the rushing waters both outside and inside his house. He woke his family and with Thomas junior clinging to him he and his wife moved towards the door to get out. At that instant the force of the water battered down the door and a second wave knocked Catherine over, still clinging to her husband's nightshirt which was ripped from his body. With Thomas junior still clinging to him, the naked Thomas Halbert managed to get them both out and to higher ground. As he returned hoping to rescue his wife and the other two children, the front wall of the house collapsed, and Thomas Halbert was knocked down by falling debris. Unable to reach his wife Catherine and the two children John and Mary Jane, they were all drowned.

Thomas Halbert claimed £300 for the loss of life of his wife and two children and was awarded £50. For his second claim of £49 9s for personal property, clothing and funeral expenses he was awarded £15 in January 1865.

The graves of the two children have not been traced.

Catherine Hallbert, recorded as aged 25, was buried in the Nonconformist area of the Cemetery on 15 March in plot MM 25, a public grave with no memorial stone.

Next door to the Halberts lived Thomas Fairhurst, a furnace man at the Philadelphia Works on Bacon Island, with his wife Ann and their four children: Sarah Elizabeth, aged 9. Mary Ann, aged 7, Fred, aged 5 and one-year-old John, also known as Thomas. As the Flood hit Neepsend Thomas was at work and on becoming aware of what was happening, rushed towards home to try and save his family. He got no further than Neepsend Bridge when he got caught up in the Flood water and drowned. Fortunately, his wife and children managed to escape the Flood and moved to Bridgehouses.

When the Coroner John Webster began to hold the inquests into the victims of the Flood, he realised that it would take weeks to hold separate inquests on all the deceased and that this could lead to a high risk of disease from decaying bodies. It was clear that they had all died by the same means so he decided to hold inquests on just four bodies which would be representative of all those who died. One of the bodies selected was that of Thomas Fairhurst.

At the inquest Ann Fairhurst said:

> The deceased Thomas Fairest (sic) is my husband. He was a furnaceman at Mr. Butcher's works. He was 47 years of age. He was drowned whilst crossing the stone bridge when he was coming home to save me and my children from the flood.
>
> *Sheffield Daily Telegraph*, 14 March 1864

Ann Fairhurst claimed £400 for the loss of her husband's life on behalf of herself and their children and she was awarded £158, Sarah Elizabeth, aged 9, received £30, Mary Ann, aged 7, received £35, Fred, aged 5, received £40 and John, also known as Thomas, aged 1, received £50.

Thomas Fairhurst, aged 47, was buried in the Anglican area of the Cemetery on 14 March in plot M3 21, a public grave with no memorial stone.

Also in the Mills Buildings, the other side of the Halberts, lived 42-year -old Thomas Peters, his wife, 33-year-old Jane and their four children: Jane, aged 10, Mary Alice, aged 7; Julia, aged 4, and Christopher, 21 months. Thomas Peters, a leather dresser, was in Lincolnshire and away from home on the night of the Flood, but Jane Peters, on being awakened by the noise of the water, woke her children and told them to follow her out of the house. They all got outside before the house filled with water, but three of the children were swept away by the force of the water and were drowned. Jane Peters and Mary Alice managed to escape the water and get to a neighbour's house.

Jane, aged 10, Julia, aged 4, Christopher Peters, aged 21 months, were buried in the Nonconformist area of the Cemetery on 14 March in plot E 153, a public grave with no memorial stone.

Thomas Peters' claim for £100 for the loss of the lives of his three children was assessed at just £15 and his claim for £16 3d for personal property and clothes was assessed at £10 10s in July 1865.

Close by, three generations of the Bright family lived at the Woolpack Inn and the adjacent terrace property. At the Inn 57-year-old Jeremiah Bright, a leather dresser, lived with his wife Mary, also 57, and their son 13-year-old Alfred. Next door lived the couple's other son, Thomas Bright, a 31-year-old leather dresser, his wife Sarah, neé Wadkins, aged 29, and their three children, Mary, aged 7, Eliza, aged 4 and 7-months-old Fanny. Thomas Bright was away from home on the night of the Flood but when the water entered the house, Sarah Bright managed to carry the baby Fanny away to safety. Mary Bright, her son Alfred, and granddaughters Mary and Eliza clung together in a corner of a bedroom and screamed for help as the Flood waters rose, too terrified to try to escape. The force of the Flood washed away the whole length of the front wall of the terrace, exposing the rooms behind it. As the waters rose higher and higher, the entire house was swept away and the four people cowering in it were drowned. The body of seven-year-old Mary was never found.

Alfred Bright, aged 13, and Eliza Bright, aged 4, were buried in the Anglican area of the Cemetery on 13 March in plot Q2 144, a public grave with no memorial stone.

Mary Bright, aged 57, was buried in the Anglican area of the Cemetery on 14 March in plot Q2 126, a public grave with no memorial stone.

Jeremiah Bright claimed £200 for the loss of his son Alfred and received a derisory £20, just ten percent of his claim. For his claim for £500 for the loss of his wife Mary, again Jeremiah Bright received ten percent of his claim, just £50.

Jeremiah Bright died in January 1866 and by 1871 Thomas Bright, his wife Sarah and baby Fanny had moved to Surrey where Thomas continued working as a leather dresser.

In a house on Orchard Street, John Vaughan, a 64-year-old grinder who rented a grinding station at the Soho Grinding Wheel, and his wife 53-year-old Elizabeth were sleeping in a ground floor room with lodgers occupying the rooms above. At ground level the couple were much more vulnerable to the rising waters and John and Elizabeth Vaughan both drowned as the Flood waters filled their bedroom to the ceiling, whilst residents on higher floors survived.

John, aged 64, and Elizabeth Vaughan, aged 53, were buried in the Nonconformist area of the Cemetery on 14 March in plot MM 42, a public grave with no memorial stone.

Three of John Vaughan's extended family acted as his administrators and put in a claim for his possessions, clothing and funeral expenses for £55 10s and received £15.

As well as the homes of local people, many small businesses suffered greatly due to the Flood. They had properties damaged, lost stock, production time and trade, plus had a much-reduced local market due to the deaths and dispersal of local residents. Neepsend was a largely industrial area with mills, tanneries, gas works and a brewery. All were badly affected. Tanneries lost many thousands of skins and pelts as the Flood water swept through and many toxic substances used in the tanning process such as dog faeces, vitriol, shumac, lime and alkali were spilled into the river, adding to the stench and pollution. The Philadelphia Works and James Dixon's Cornish Works all suffered extensive damage as the wall of water continued towards the centre of Sheffield, demolishing the Ball Street Bridge, spreading over both banks of the Don and over Kelham Island.

In a yard in nearby Long Croft lived the Colton family who slept in a ground floor room that was filled to the ceiling by the Flood water.

> In Long Croft, between Green Lane and the river, several persons lost their lives. In a yard here lived Christoper Colton, his wife, and a sister's child, aged five years. They slept on the ground floor, and were aroused by the water lifting up the beds in which they had been reposing. They got up, and rushed to the door; but it would not open even with their most desperate exertions. The water held the door tight, and was every moment rising higher and higher. They screamed out for help, but no help came, and they were drowned in the room, which was completely filled with water up to the ceiling.
>
> *A Complete History of the Great Flood of Sheffield,* Samuel Harrison, 1864

Christopher and Mary Colton, aged 46 and 30 respectively, were buried in the Anglican area of the Cemetery on 14 March in plot Q2 144, a public grave with no memorial stone.

Christopher Colton's sons by a previous marriage claimed £46 10s for damage to their father's personal property plus funeral expenses and were awarded £11 11s.

VIEW FROM THE BALL STREET BRIDGE, SHEFFIELD.

On Kelham Street, the Sheffield Union Workhouse, a former cotton mill and home to about 1,200 residents, was swamped by water coming through the sewers and the doors, to a depth of about four feet. At this distance from Dale Dyke the power of the Flood was declining and there was little structural damage, but the waters brought mud, debris and pollution into the building. For the residents, many of whom were vulnerable, sick or disabled, it was a horrific experience. Fortunately, everyone remained calm, those on the ground floor were directed to a higher level where they were safe and there was no loss of life.

Emma Walliss, a widow, lived on Cotton Mill Row a narrow lane between Alma Street and Bower Street behind the Workhouse with two of her children, 11-year-old Clara Amelia and 5-year-old Herbert James.

In Cotton Mill Row, near Alma Street, lived a poor old widow woman named Wallace (sic), along with her two children. She only occupied one small room, and that was on the ground floor below the level of Alma Street. When the flood rushed into the house, she got out of bed, burst open the door, and went outside into the water. But she could get no further, and all she could do was to scream out for assistance. In the same house other families lived in the upstairs rooms, and one of them opened the window to see if they could rescue the poor old woman. A young man threw out a sheet and told her to seize hold of it. She did so, and the young man pulled the sheet till she was just within his reach, but at that moment a rush of water carried her away. She gave one piercing scream, and was heard no more. Her dead body was afterwards found in a yard adjoining. Her two children, whom she had left in bed, were bravely rescued by a man named Whiteley.

A Complete History of the Great Flood of Sheffield, Samuel Harrison, 1864

Emma Walliss, aged 47, was buried in the Nonconformist area of the Cemetery on 15 March in plot NN 25, a public grave with no memorial stone.

A claim was made on the loss of the life of Emma Walliss on behalf of her children for £500. The paltry sum of £32 was awarded. The claim for the damage to her personal property, her and her children's clothing and her funeral expenses was £46 17s 10d with just £15 being awarded in June 1865.

The main force of the Flood continued along the River Don, demolishing bridges, ruining livelihoods, although its main power had lessened as it left Neepsend behind. Beyond the Wicker the railway station was flooded and in an office at the coal wharf slept John Thornton Peacock a 63-year-old bookkeeper from Wickersley who drowned.

John Thornton Peacock, aged 63, was buried in the Nonconformist area of the Cemetery on 15 March in plot F 28, a public grave with no memorial stone.

The Flood water continued through Attercliffe, Tinsley and on towards Rotherham and Doncaster. Its power diminished, the only evidence of the Flood being the unusual and quickly rising water levels of the Don and the huge amount of timber, uprooted trees, animal carcasses, broken furniture and other debris carried along and dumped on the banksides. Cellars were flooded but it was the environmental damage that was most significant with the noxious water polluting the land and several corpses needing to be recovered.

The Aftermath

Recovery of the Bodies

The morning of 12 March 1864 was clear and bright and very much in contrast to the preceding day. A chance for residents to realise the enormity of the previous day's events and to take stock of what had been lost.

In the afternoon of 12 March in the boardroom of the Sheffield Union Workhouse, the Coroner, John Webster, opened the Inquest into the deaths of Thomas and Elizabeth Elston, Keziah Eaton and Thomas Fairhurst who were the victims who would represent all who perished in the Flood caused by the failure of the Dale Dyke dam. After viewing the bodies and interviewing the witnesses who found them, the bodies were released for burial.

During the following days, bodies were retrieved from the debris left by the receding waters, dug out of the mud and taken to various public houses, prominent buildings and the Sheffield Workhouse. In Rotherham, 15 miles away, 13 bodies were recovered and several more in Doncaster, over 27 miles from the Dale Dyke Dam. Posters and the local press urged people with missing loved ones to visit the makeshift mortuaries, identify their loved ones and take them away for burial.

At the Sheffield Union Workhouse 124 unclaimed bodies arrived and the Board of Guardians made arrangements for them to be washed, laid out on straw covered by a white cloth and labelled as they were identified.

The Scene at the Workhouse.

> The scene was most harrowing. The dead lay in rows in five adjoining rooms. The bereaved hurried from room to room, scanning the countenances of the dead, with tremulous anxiety. Some in their eagerness and excitement passed their friends several times before recognising them. Others identified them at a glance. All appeared deeply distressed. Some of the women wrung their hands and beat their fists together in in-expressible agony at the sight of dear ones who had been so suddenly snatched away. Others knelt beside the corpses of husbands, brothers, or children, kissed their cold faces over and over again, bedewing them with streaming tears, clutching their cold clasped hands and sobbing as if their hearts would break. Others were to be seen cutting off locks, to preserve as precious memorials of those most dear to them. Altogether the scene was heart-rending.
>
> *Sheffield and Rotherham Independent* , 15 March 1864

For people who could afford to inter their dead, the bodies were given up as soon as they were identified, the Guardians lending coffins for their removal. For some who could ill afford the expense but were keen to bury their friends, financial aid was given by the Guardians and for those too poor to undertake the interment at all, the Guardians arranged to inter at the expense of the Sheffield Union. In both cases friends could choose the burial ground to be used and they were given notice of the time of the interment so that they had the opportunity to be present.

Identification and Burial of the Dead

The unidentified bodies were interred at the General Cemetery by the Guardians at the expense of the Sheffield Union. Several bodies were sent to the Cemetery at the same time, but the burials did not attract any public attention and there were very few spectators. The *Sheffield and Rotherham Independent* of 15 March 1864 reported:

> They were not all interred in one particular area of the Cemetery, but in separate graves in different parts according to circumstances, the interments being conducted with all the decencies and solemnity of private interments.

Burial of the dead in the Cemetery began on Sunday 13 March when three of the victims were interred. Monday 14 March witnessed 13 burials and on Tuesday 15 March, 37 bodies were brought to the Cemetery and placed in the ground.

Relief Fund

For those who had lost everything bar the nightclothes on their backs, relief had to be sought immediately through the generosity of family, friends and neighbours.

The authorities had to act quickly to deliver an official structure of relief and reduce the level of misery caused by the Flood. At a meeting of many of the town's public figures on Monday 14 March the process of raising subscriptions was begun, pledges made and by the end of the meeting £4,775 had been donated. The following day a formal committee was appointed to raise money for the relief of the needy and to oversee its distribution. Every working man in Sheffield was asked to donate a day's wages, something that many could ill afford, but such was the enormity of the disaster most wanted to do all they could to relieve the suffering.

Initially, even when relief was made available, lack of communication and supply channels meant that it was not always received quickly by those most in need as told in these excerpts from the *Sheffield and Rotherham Independent* of 16 March 1864.

> The houses of all who had escaped were thrown open, and hundreds of men, women, and children, nearly all in their night clothes only, were taken through the sea of mud that surrounded the villages, and supplied with the best food and shelter that the humble means of their neighbours could command. Their condition was most deplorable, and unfortunately, although both men and women borrowed clothes of all kinds from their friends wherewith to clothe the sufferers, the supply fell far short of the demand, and women and children were exposed for many hours to bitter discomforts which cannot be appreciated until they have been endured. One of the severest sources of suffering was the inability to provide fires in the houses that were left standing. The cellars were filled with mud, which rendered the stock of coals inaccessible.
>
> An elderly woman, named Hibberd, who had supported herself and her daughter by selling barm*, and whose house was a mere shell filled with mud and stones, came up the path, and, wringing her hands in utter despair, exclaimed "Nothing until to-morrow!" She had been to request relief, and was told to come again "tomorrow." She had no shoes, and, what was more important, she had no bread.

*barm, the froth on the top of fermenting liquids such as beer

One great necessity, after the want of bread, was the want of shoes. Generally, the people had left their shoes and boots in the lower rooms when they went to bed on the Friday night, and they were of course swept away with the other contents of those rooms. Yesterday, in Haydon's row, in the only house that is now inhabited, we saw a family named Smith. The children (four or five in number) were oddly attired in any sort of clothes that had come to hand; their mother had no shoes, and was trampling in the mud with only pieces of rag around her feet. She seemed to be completely ignorant that any means of relief had been made available until that afternoon, when her husband had got several loaves given to him. She said she "wouldn't care if she could only get a pair of boots, so that she could go about."

Mrs Elizabeth Hoole, a widow, who has maintained her family with the assistance of her daughter, by washing and mangling* and who has been one of the severest sufferers amongst the poorer inhabitants, applied to Mr Dearden for relief. She appeared to be utterly destitute. Her house was a perfect wreck, and the family had escaped almost by a miracle. Mrs Hoole said Mr. Dearden had told her she did not belong to his parish, and therefore he could not relieve her. We believe her house, or the mass of mud, capped by a few slates, that occupies the place where the house stood, is out of the district which was placed under Mr. Dearden's charge. Mr. Hoole's daughter was trying to wash, in front of the house a few articles of clothing that she had got out of the mud; and she told us that the clothing she was wearing was borrowed. Her little sister was stood shivering against the wall of mud in a ragged frock and petticoat.

*mangling, squeezing water out of material

Another great cause of suffering arose because of the damage to the works and manufactories and the destruction of the workmen's tools. Many people were unable to return to their employment which impacted on families' incomes.

The Sheffield Flood was recognised nationally with nearly every town in Britain contributing and Queen Victoria making a personal donation of £200. By the end of April, the committee reported that over £50,000 had been raised and 20,537 people had received relief of some kind, the money being spent on food, clothing, 4,000 pairs of shoes, furniture and workmen's tools. It was also reported that 4,357 houses had been flooded, 798 had been destroyed and abandoned, 11 wives were now widows, 40 children had been orphaned and 250 people were known to have lost their lives. By May the appeal was closed as the amount raised was considered enough to cover the immediate needs.

Swift action was also needed in clearing up the debris left by the Flood. For miles along the banks of the rivers Don and Loxley there were decaying animal bodies, broken sewers and privies and obnoxious substances from the manufactories. Prompt action by local fire brigades in pumping out cellars and the organisation of the Water Company's navvies and labourers from the Duke of Norfolk's estate into teams to clear away the debris reduced the risk of spreading infectious diseases. The only health concern that did arise was an outbreak of fever some weeks after the Flood at Owlerton but measures to stop its progress were quickly introduced.

As well as the physical needs of the distressed, their spiritual needs were addressed by organisations such as the British and Foreign Bible Society who supplied copies of bibles to families who had lost theirs in the Flood.

Sightseers and Photographers

As the news spread of the terrible events of the previous night, many people went to view the Dale Dyke dam and the route of the Flood. Some went to offer assistance in whatever way they could, others just went to look. It was estimated that within the next few days 150,000 Sheffielders were to view the devastation and as many again travelled from other towns and villages. Photographers were out in force, producing postcards as souvenirs, as were people hunting among the muddy debris for items as mementoes.

> On Monday last thousands inspected the ruins of Malin-bridge. From Hillsbro' to Bacon Island, the road had the appearance of a fair. The large number of persons congregated here was no doubt occasioned by the fine view which could be obtained of the desolation in that part of Neepsend lying round the Fairfield Hotel. The weather was beautifully clear, scarcely a cloud flitted across the azure sky, and the country might be seen for a considerable distance. The terrible destruction inflicted by the flood was distinctly observable. The inhabitants of the houses about this district are busily engaged pumping the water out of their cellars ; and on lines in gardens at the back hang carpets, mattress-cases, and other things which have been saturated by the flood.

The newspaper went on:

> The appearance of the streets this day was that of some of the busiest thoroughfares in the metropolis. Thousands of persons poured in from all parts of the country, and vehicles of every description, from a brougham to a mere donkey cart, were employed to convey the spectators to the moor. Omnibuses also ran from the town to Hillsbro', which bore large tickets

> with the words 'To Hillsbro' and the ruins', and countless were the passengers who availed themselves of them. From Bridgehouse through the narrow lanes to Harvestland poured one continuous stream of all grades of society.
>
> *Doncaster, Nottingham and Lincoln Gazette*, 18 March 1864

Laurence Frederick Peacock (1838-1900) was one of the photographers who went to view and record the devastation. Born in Leeds to Thomas and Ann Peacock, by 1851 the family were living in Paradise Square, Sheffield with Thomas working as a dealer in cutlery. Laurence Peacock married Arabella Turner in 1859 and the couple had at least 5 children.

In 1861 Laurence and Arabella Peacock were living on New Cemetery Road with their one-year-old daughter, Emma Jane. After the Flood, Peacock took his darkroom out with him and recorded the pathway of the water from Dale Dyke down into the town. He used the glass slides he created to illustrate talks about his experience and his script and some of his slides survive.

> …I will again draw your attention to my dark room as I have previously explained it ran on 4 wheels but when I had a long journey to go I engaged a donkey and cart and lifted the dark room onto the cart which made it much easier travelling. You will perceive the turnout on the road behind the ruins. My carriage and pair - I mean dark room with donkey and cart, you must remember the roads were very bad to traverse being full of large stones and bricks and having deep holes washed in them by the force of the water. All the bridges being washed away and the rivers had to be forded, now it is well known that

donkeys as a rule have a way of their own and if they think won't – they won't, now our donkey was no exception to this rule and when he came to the water at Bradfield he thought he wouldn't cross – and he wouldn't. The water was three feet or three feet six inches deep and about 50 navvies were at work round about, some getting the foundations for the new bridge and others were building boundary walls. After having a good laugh at our predicament one of them came to me and offered along with his mates to carry the whole lot across for half a crown, donkey, cart, dark room and three passengers, they got some poles and putting one through both wheels and 2 under the donkey, a man on either end of each pole, that is 10 men carried the whole lot across then 3 of them returned for my boy, the driver and myself we mounted their backs and were taken across the water and so we proceeded on our journey to the broken reservoir, this carrying procedure had to be repeated on the return home.

Bradfield Archives

In the census of 1881 Peacock appears to have been recorded twice. Laurence Frederick Peacock, Photographers Assistant, aged 42 was recorded as living at 2 Victoria Street, Sheffield with his wife Arabella and their two children. Frederick Peacock, Photographer, aged 40 was recorded as living in Whittington, Derbyshire with his wife Henrietta and their two children.

Peacock's first wife Arabella died in June 1883 and later that year he married Henrietta Wildgoose. Peacock and his second wife also had at least five children before Henrietta's death in December 1885. Peacock married Eliza Botfield in March 1894. Eliza had been a 21-year-old domestic servant in Peacock's household in 1891.

Laurence Frederick Peacock died in May 1900 and was buried in the Nonconformist area of the Cemetery in plot T 109, a public grave.
His parents, first two wives and five of his children were buried in the Nonconformist area of the Cemetery in plot S 183.

The remains of Turner Wheel, Malin Bridge, Hillsborough with the dark room of Mr. Peacock, the photographer on a cart pulled by a donkey in the background

Aftermath Victims

John Marriott, a carter, and his wife Mary had lived on Spring Street with their four daughters until Mary Marriott died in July 1861. When John Marriott died on 29 March 1864 it is believed he succumbed to an illness directly caused by the Flood. Certainly the "loss of life" claim by his daughter Ellen Marriott was settled by the Inundation Commissioners so they were satisfied his death was the result of the Flood, although the claim for £300 was assessed at a miserly £5. Ellen Marriott's other claim for furniture and household effects for £3 17s 6d was withdrawn.

John Marriott, aged 61, was buried on 3 April in the Nonconformist area of the Cemetery, plot NN 48, a public grave with no stone.

Alfred Huddlestone, a veterinary surgeon, and his wife Mary Ann Huddlestone were badly injured in the Flood and Mary Ann died a little over four months later. The fact that Alfred Huddlestone was successfully able to make a claim against the Waterworks Company suggests that it was acknowledged that Mary Ann Huddlestone was a victim of the Flood.

Mary Ann Huddlestone, aged 59, was buried on 2 August in the Consecrated area of the Cemetery, plot Z2 153.

Alfred Huddlestone claimed £100 for his wife's surgeon's bill, funeral expenses, nursing care and "the loss of her services" and was awarded £25. He also claimed £50 for the surgeon attending him, having to go away to the seaside and being unable to work due to being unwell. He was awarded £50. Huddlestone died four years later and was buried in the same grave as his wife. The stone memorialised three of their children, two of whom predeceased them.

In August 1864 workmen near Attercliffe Bridge uncovered a body which was thought to be that of a victim of the Flood:

> About three o'clock on Monday afternoon, some men who were digging sand near the Attercliffe-bridge, discovered the body of a man. The remains were in a shocking state of decomposition, and are presumed to be those of one of the victims of the disastrous flood which occurred on the 12th of March last. They were shovelled into a box and information of the discovery was conveyed to the police, who obtained a coffin from the Workhouse, placed the remains therein and then removed them to the General Cemetery, where they will be interred to-day.
>
> *Sheffield Daily Telegraph,* 20 August 1864

The unidentified body was buried on 16 August in the Nonconformist area of the Cemetery, plot E 133, a public grave with no memorial stone.

Aaron Dearden, a member of the firm of Messrs Rodgers and Dearden at Philadelphia Corn Mills and active in public life, serving on education and housing committees in the Nether Hallam ward, had a number of tragedies in his life. In September 1851 his 19-month-old son, George

> … wandered unobserved into the shop where his father worked, and by some means its frock became entangled with a drum, which was then revolving with great velocity. The child was drawn between the strap and the drum, and crushed in a fearful manner.
>
> *Sheffield Independent*, 27 September 1851

In March 1864 Dearden was living in a house on the premises of the Corn Mill with his family when the Flood struck. The mill and their house were flooded, the lower rooms being fully under water which also rose up into the bedrooms. Aaron Dearden, his wife Elizabeth and their children escaped through a window and clung on to the roof of their home for several hours before the waters subsided and they could be rescued. Dearden's anxiety for his family coupled with the severe cold he caught as a result of the exposure he suffered that night had a serious impact on his health. He claimed £250 compensation for 16 weeks of medical treatment for "shock to the Nervous System from the Flood" during which he was unable to work. He was awarded £77 2s.

The Dearden family moved to Albert Terrace Road but every year, as the anniversary of the Flood came round, Aaron Dearden had a bout of depression which left him in a very weakened state. So regular was the depression that according to the *Sheffield Independent* of 3 July 1879 he used to refer to it as "his annual attack of flood fever". Aaron and Elizabeth Dearden lost their 21-year-old daughter Elizabeth in 1868 and Dearden's wife died in 1875. Six months later his mills were destroyed by fire and although the buildings were insured, the stock was not. The financial loss to the business was substantial. His attack of "flood fever" in 1879 was particularly severe and he told friends that "he really felt tired of his life". Instead of getting better his depression increased and one morning in July when his daughter went to his bedroom to take him his breakfast, she found him lying on the floor with his neck tied by his handkerchief to one of the posts at the foot of the bed and having a deep cut on his left wrist from which he had lost a large amount of blood. A doctor was called, and Aaron Dearden was pronounced dead.

Aaron Dearden, aged 61, died on 2 July 1879 and was buried in the Nonconformist area of the Cemetery in plots EE 152/153. Also buried in the plots were his daughters Elizabeth and Fanny and wife Elizabeth. There is no memorial stone.

Newspaper Reporting

Samuel Harrison was born in Somerset, the son of a Wesleyan minister, and after attending Woodhouse Grove School in Bradford arrived in Sheffield as an apprentice in the printing trade. Living and working on High Street at a bookseller and stationer, Harrison taught himself shorthand and gained a position as reporter on *The Sheffield Times,* a weekly paper, where a fellow reporter was Henry Pawson. When the owner of the paper, William Willot, retired in 1854 the two men went into partnership and bought it from him. The partnership was dissolved in 1857 as Pawson was more interested in the commercial printing and stationery part of the business. Samuel Harrison took on new premises on Bow Street where he introduced new techniques which helped to revolutionise newspaper printing. His methods improved standards and increased circulation figures plus enabled the business to get news out to the public as quickly as possible. Samuel Harrison had married Mary Gardner in 1853 and by 1861 the couple were living on Gell Street with their five children, all under seven years old, and Harrison was employing 36 people.

At the time of the Sheffield Flood and working with William Leng, the editor of *The Sheffield Daily Telegraph*, reporters were sent out in the middle of the night to gather stories, enabling people to read accurate reports of the disaster the next morning. Further editions followed during the day keeping people updated whilst other towns further afield also received copy. Samuel Harrison followed up many of the distressing stories that emerged over the following weeks, checking them and compiling them into the complete story of the Flood from the building of the dam to the paying of compensation. *A Complete History of the Great Flood of Sheffield on March 11 and 12, 1864*, originally printed in 1864 was reprinted in 1898 as *The Great Sheffield Flood Its*

History Retold and again in 1974 as *A Complete History of the Great Flood at Sheffield.* Copies of the book were, and still are, cherished by generations of Sheffielders, particularly those with family connections to the Flood and to those wanting to learn more about the events of that time. Indeed this present book draws on some of the details in Harrison's work.

Samuel and Mary Harrison's thirteenth child, William Walter, was born in March 1870 but lived only a few hours. Their fourteenth child, Caroline, was born on 4 February 1871 but died just 24 hours later. Samuel Harrison's death on 21 February of the same year, at his home Oak Villa on Clark House Road, from a "fever" followed by bronchitis, came as a real shock to his family and people who knew and respected him for his tireless work ethic. At the age of 44 and with his remaining ten children under sixteen years of age he would have been expected to live a much longer life.

Samuel Harrison, aged 44, was buried on 25 February 1871 in the Anglican area of the Cemetery in plot H 50. His wife Mary, daughters Caroline, Charlotte Helena and Mary Edith, and sons John James and William Walter were also buried in the plot.
Sons George Heath and Albert Charles, daughter Annie Louisa and a second son called William Walter, were memorialised on the gravestone but not buried in the plot.

Compensation Claims

Whilst the short-term issues were adequately dealt with by the relief appeal, there were claims against the Water Company for compensation for the loss of family members, property and expenses incurred because of the Flood. An Act of Parliament gave powers to the Sheffield Waterworks Company to raise the water rates by 25% to fulfil the compensation claims. 7,300 claims totalling £458,552 were made and £275,000 was paid out.

The claims were assessed by three Inundation Commissioners who had the task of awarding the compensation. Not all the claims were valid, some were downright fraudulent and not everyone made a claim, possibly because they did not know how to, they could not read and write or maybe there was nobody left behind to make a claim.

The claims, which are now available online at www.shu.ac.uk/sfca/, detail the furniture, clothes, books, toys, household utensils and goods of the victims of the Flood. They show that while the Commissioners assumed that property could be valued, the significance of a human life was valued in terms of the loss of earning power, with nothing given for personal grief and anguish. Little compensation was awarded for the loss of a relative unless they were the breadwinner, and the lives of many of the women and children were assessed as having insignificant value. The worth put on human lives ranged from £5 to £1,000, the wealthy appearing to fare much better than the poor. Many people, having lost everything they possessed except the clothes on their backs, received miserly amounts of money with very few of the claimants receiving the full amount claimed. Walter George Sykes, a powder flask manufacturer of Moorgate Rotherham, received over £487 for the loss of books and papers whilst William Coggin, a tanner of Neepsend, received just £25 after the loss of his three children.

Inquest and Reports

When the Coroner's Inquest resumed on 23 March several theories were put forward as to the cause of the collapse of the dam wall, but the evidence was inconclusive. Clearly mistakes had been made in the construction of the reservoir and the design could have been better, but no criminal proceedings were taken against the Waterworks Company or its engineers.

A Government Inspector was sent from London to make a thorough investigation into the causes of the Flood and their report was damning, suggesting that the design of the embankment was flawed, and criticising the method of construction and the selection of materials. The professional standards of the Waterworks Company's engineers were also questioned. The Sheffield Waterworks Company commissioned their own report into the dam's failure and that concluded that the collapse of the dam was due to a landslide and "an unavoidable accident". Sheffield Corporation's report agreed with that of the Government Inspector, the failure resulted from faulty construction.

John Gunson (1809–1886) appeared before the Government Inspector as the Resident Engineer of the Sheffield Waterworks Company as he was responsible for the construction of the Dale Dyke reservoir. He was born in Hunslet, Leeds, had married Charlotte Simpson in 1831 and joined the Waterworks Company in the same year. Gunson was a devoted and conscientious worker and supervised the building of the Rivelin, Dale Dyke (original and current), Agden, Strines and Dam Flask reservoirs. The couple had three sons and a daughter and at the time of the Flood Gunson, aged 54, was living on Division Street at its junction with Carver Lane, next door to the Company's Offices. He was never to forget that horrific night on the moors above Bradfield or the sight of the destruction and plight of those who suffered. He was the one who came under most criticism from the Government Inspector, but the Waterworks Company stood by him and he remained in their employment for the rest of his life.

John Gunson, engineer, Sheffield Water Company, 1880

Even late in his life, when his health deteriorated and he was unable to go to his office, he worked from home and colleagues continued to seek his advice due to his vast knowledge of the company's affairs.

John Gunson died at his home at Clarkson Street on 10 October 1886, having worked for the Company for 55 years. For 22 of those years, Gunson, a person of a "singularly retiring disposition" had carried with him the massive memory of the collapse of the Dale Dyke dam. "The perils of that night and the terrible results of the catastrophe, were ever vividly remembered by him": according to the *Sheffield Telegraph* of 12 October 1886.

John Gunson, aged 77, was buried on 14 October 1886, in the Nonconformist area of the Cemetery in plot H 146. His wife Charlotte and two grandchildren were also buried in the plot.

The Legacy

The rebuilding of the physical environment quickly got underway with new roads, bridges and buildings appearing and the damaged ones being repaired. Emotionally and physically, it took a long time for people to heal, if indeed they ever did. For many, the scars remained for the rest of their lives.

Sheffield was still in need of an increased water supply and in 1875 a new embankment was built a few hundred yards upstream and with an improved design, yet it was a further 12 years before the reservoir served its original purpose of supplying clean water to Sheffield. In January 1888 Sheffield Corporation took over the Sheffield Waterworks Company and in 1974 Sheffield's water supply was transferred to the newly created Yorkshire Water Authority. In 1989 the Conservative Government put Yorkshire Water back into private ownership.

Memorials

At the time of the Flood there was a call for a monument to be erected to those lost and Samuel Harrison suggested that the remainder of the Relief Fund money should be used for installing a permanent memorial. This did not happen and instead it was proposed that any surplus money should be returned to the donors! 50 years later, his son, Councillor S Gardner Harrison commented in the *Sheffield Daily Telegraph* of 11 March 1914:

> I have made inquiries and believe it to be the fact that no monument or memorial exists in connection with the Flood. It is late in the day to suggest such a thing, nevertheless would it not be well if some modest cenotaph were erected in some

> convenient place, say, in the General Cemetery, where many of the victims were buried? … A calamity such as burst upon Sheffield just fifty years ago to-day ought to have its fitting memorial.

Today a memorial in St Polycarp's Church at Malin Bridge which was created soon after the Flood lists the names of some who died. It was originally in the chapel at the bottom of Loxley Road, moved initially to St Mark's Church, Dykes Lane and then to St Polycarp's Church when it was first built.

A memorial above Bradfield, unveiled by the Bradfield Historical Society on the 127th anniversary of the Flood, stands dedicated to the lives lost. Nearby are four "CLOB" stones [Centre Line of the Old Bank], two on each side of the river, marking the position of the original dam, downstream of the present structure.

At various other points along the Flood route there are commemorative stones and plaques referencing the event. This includes a memorial inscribed with the names of the victims unveiled in 2008 at Millsands on the Upper Don Trail where flowers are laid on each anniversary.

The 27 unidentified victims of the Sheffield Flood who were buried in Sheffield General Cemetery were buried in public graves with no stones but in 2023 a memorial plaque to these unidentified people, sixteen of them children, was installed as part of the Heritage Lottery funded improvements.

Appendices

Extract from "A Retrospect of the Great Sheffield Flood"

The Bradfield waters calm reposed
Where verdant hills the dam o'er look.
When, suddenly, a mighty crash
The village from its slumbers shook.
The Reservoir its banks had burst,
Oh God! That wild tumultuous roar!
The torrent rushed with frantic speed,
Grim death, destruction to outpour.

Huge stones and trees were overthrown,
As by an avalanche uptorn,
The surging flood o'er Loxley swept,
And swift to Malin Bridge was borne.
'Twas bleak and dark when shrieks and prayers
Arose upon the midnight air,
Tempestuous billows mocked the cries
Of the scores of souls who perished there.

Ah! the piteous sight of youth and age,
The feeble sire and father brave,
Poor mother with the babe new-born,
And children tossed upon the wave.
Farms, cattle and flocks were swept away
As on to Hillsbro' rushed the tide;
To Neepsend Bridge from Owlerton,
Beyond the Wicker spreading wide.

Some victims tried – though some in vain,
To mount an attic, roof or tree;
What tragic memories long would cling
To the desperate folk who struggled free.
We hear of near escapes from death,
Of peril and exposure braved,
Of families in their sore distress
By noble deed of rescue saved.

But oh! The havoc of the tide,
The miles of devastation wrought,
Well nigh a thousand homes were wrecked
And thousands more the deluge caught.
Machines and engines ruined lay;
Shops, stocks and stores were overthrown,
A score of bridges swept away.

But how describe the scenes next day,
The mangled wrecks entombed in mud,
The children's cries, the fireless grate
Of starving folk marooned by flood.
Appalling was the aftermath,
A thousand piteous tales were heard,
Relief poured in spontaneously,
Full deep a Nation's heart was stirred.

The Malin Church a tablet bears,
No public monument is reared,
Just tombstones in God's Acres stand,
With loving thoughts of those endeared –
Time speeds more, memory lingers on,
Where the Bradfield Reservoirs now lie,
Serene, 'mid everlasting hills,
A constant bountiful supply.

Ellen Styring, Woodseats, 1947

Victims buried in Sheffield General Cemetery

Ang = Anglican area, NC = Nonconformist area

13 March 1864		
	Bright, Alfred	Ang, Q2 144, public grave
	Bright, Eliza	Ang, Q2 144, public grave
	Gilyatt, Susan	Ang, M3 21, public grave
14 March 1864		
	Bright, Mary	Ang, Q2 126, public grave
	Coggin, Alfred	Ang, G2 126, public grave
	Coggin, Eliza	Ang, G2 126, public grave
	Coggin, William	Ang, G2 126, public grave
	Colton, Christopher	Ang, Q2 144, public grave
	Colton, Mary	Ang, Q2 144, public grave
	Fairhurst, Thomas	Ang, M3 21, public grave
	Peters, Christopher	NC, E 153, public grave
	Peters, Jane	NC, E 153, public grave
	Peters, Julia	NC, E 153, public grave
	Snape, George	Ang, Q2 128, public grave
	Vaughan, Elizabeth	NC, MM 42, public grave
	Vaughan, John	NC, MM 42, public grave
15 March 1864		
	Appleby, Mary	Ang, B3 175
	Gannon, John	NC, MM 42, public grave
	Gannon, Sarah	NC, MM 42, public grave
	Gannon, William	NC, MM 46, public grave
	Gannon, Henry	NC, MM 76, public grave
	Gannon, Peter	NC, MM 56, public grave
	Gannon, Margaret	NC, MM 27, public grave
	Halbert, Catherine	NC, MM 25, public grave
	Midwood, George	Ang, T2 2, public grave
	Midwood, Pheobe	Ang, Q2 136, public grave
	Marshall, Herbert Gravenor	NC, LL 69
	Peacock, John T	NC, F 28, public grave
	Pearson, Ann	Ang, M3 21, public grave
	Pickering, Charlotte	NC, G 120
	Pickering, Elizabeth	NC, G 120

	Turton, John	Ang, Q2 138, public grave
	Turton, Susan	Ang, Q2 138, public grave
	Walliss, Emma	NC, NN 25, public grave
	No 1, Male Child	NC, F 29, public grave
	No 2, Male Child	NC, N 40, public grave
	No 3, Male Child	NC, F 30, public grave
	No 4, Child	Ang, G2 114, public grave
	No 5, Female Child	Ang, Q2 138, public grave
	No 6, Child	Ang, G2 114, public grave
	No 7, Male Child	NC, MM 56, public grave
	No 8, Female Child	Ang, T2 4, public grave
	No 9, Female Adult	NC, N 40, public grave
	No 10, Female Child	NC, F 29, public grave
	No 11, Child	Ang, Q2 138, public grave
	No 12, Male Child	NC, NN 86, public grave
	No 13, Male Child	NC, E 54, public grave
	No 14, Male Adult	NC, NN 86, public grave
	No 15, Male Adult	NC, MM 42, public grave
	No 16, Female Child	NC, MM 91, public grave
	No 17, Adult	Ang, Q2 136, public grave
	No 18, Female Child	Ang, T2 4, public grave
	No 19, Female unknown	Ang, Q2 136, public grave
17 March 1864		
	Appleby, John Coulton	Ang, B3 175
	Appleby, Mary	Ang, B3 175
	Female Child	NC, NN 74, public grave
	Male Child	NC, NN 74, public grave
21 March 1864		
	A Girl	NC, NN 74, public grave
	A Man	NC, MM 50, public grave
30 March 1864		
	A Boy	Ang, Q2 136, public grave
3 April 1864		
	Marriott, J	NC, NN 48, public grave
4 April 1864		
	Female Child	NC, NN 47, public grave

6 April 1864		
	A Boy unknown	Ang, G2 136, public grave
17 April 1864		
	Bethell, William	Ang X2 161, public grave
18 April 1864		
	Bethell, William – body removed to Rotherham Moorgate Cemetery at the request of his wife.	
20 April 1864		
	Longley, William	Ang, X2 140, public grave
5 May 1864		
	Bagshaw, James	Ang, G3 30, public grave
12 June 1864		
	Marshall, Harry Somerville	NC, LL 69
2 August 1864		
	Huddlestone, Mary Ann	Ang, Z2 153,
16 August 1864		
	A man found drowned at Attercliffe Bridge	NC, E 133, public grave
5 July 1879		
	Dearden, Aaron	NC, EE 152

Conversion Chart

1 stone = 6.35 kilograms
1 foot = 0.3 meters
1 yard = 0.9 metres
1 shilling = 5 pence
1 crown = 5 shillings = 25 pence

Claims made against the Sheffield Water Company

by victims buried in the Cemetery

Details at www.sheffieldfloodclaimsarchive.shu.ac.uk

	Claim		Claim made	Claim awarded
Appleby	105	Loss of life of John C Appleby	750	£200
	5983	Loss of property of John C Appleby	£98 7s 4d	£65
	106	Loss of life of Mary Appleby	£200	£12 2s
	5982	Loss of property of Mary Appleby	£10 15s 6d	£5 11s 6d
	107	Loss of life of Mary Appleby	£100	Withdrawn
	5981	Loss of property of Mary Appleby	£39 13s	£24
Bethell	56	Loss of life of William Bethell	£2650	£1000
Bright	49	Loss of life of Alfred Bright	£200	£20
	55	Loss of life of Mary Bright	£500	£50
Coggin	91	Loss of life of 3 children	£450	Withdrawn
	18	Loss of life of Alfred	£350	£25
Colton	894	Damage to property	£46 10s	£11 11s
Dearden	124	Medical expenses	£250	£77 2s
	6134	Loss of property	£187 10s	£168 15s
	4074	Damage to property	£757 7s 11d	£650
Fairhurst	24	Loss of life	£400	£313
Gilyatt	65	Loss of life of Susannah Gilyatt	50	Withdrawn
	4401	Loss of property of Susannah Gilyatt	£41 18s 6d	£12 10s
Halbert	61	Loss of life of Catherine Halbert	£300	£50
	4400	Loss of property	£49 92	£15
Huddlestone	273	Bodily injury of Mary Huddlestone	£100	£25
	275	Bodily injury of Alfred Huddlestone	£50	£50
Longley	63	Loss of life of William Longley	£300	Withdrawn
	5075	Loss of property	£20 5s	£22 7s
Marriott	38	Loss of life of John Marriott	£300	£5
	3837	Loss of property	£3 17s 6d	Withdrawn
Marshall	25	Loss of life of Herbert G Marshall	£150	£5
	3222	Loss of property	£10 17s 9d	£9
Midwood	206	Bodily injury of Joel Midwood	£5 8s	£5 18s 6d
	5146	Loss of property	£184 13s 2d	£96 3s
Peters	4	Loss of life of 3 children	£100	£15
	5382	Loss of property	£16 3d	£10 10s
	5953	Loss of property	£7 8s	Withdrawn

Pickering	58	Loss of life of Elizabeth Pickering	£41 2s 6d	£20
	59	Loss of life of William Pickering	£82 5s	£82 5s
	149	Bodily injury of Mary Ann Pickering	£20	£10
	2419	Damage to property	£4 4s	Withdraw
	4376	Loss of property	£23 1s 9d	£15
	4377	Loss of property	£5	£3
	4385	Loss of property	£243 11s 1d	£150
Snape	101	Loss of life of George Snape	£800	£110
	102	Loss of life of Mary Snape	£600	Withdrawn
	5978	Loss of property	£46 4s 8d	£20
Vaughan	5762	Loss of property	£55 10s£15	
Walliss	79	Loss of life of Emma Walliss	£500	£32
	5168	Loss of property	£46 17s 10d	£15

Sources

Amey, Geoffrey, *The Collapse of the Dale Dyke Dam 1864*, 1974

Drewry, Mick, *Inundation, The History, the Times and the People of The Great Sheffield Flood of 1864,* 2014

Harrison, Samuel, *A Complete History of the Great Flood at Sheffield*, 1864

Harrison, Samuel, *A Complete History of the Great Flood at Sheffield, with a new Foreword by Mary Walton,* 1974

Machan, Peter, *The Dramatic Story of The Sheffield Flood*, 1999

Parkin, Phil, *The Forgotten Flood,* DVD

Sheffield & Rotherham Wildlife Trust, *TORRENT: Sheffield's Flood Story*, 2022, YouTube

Sheffield City Archives, *Sheffield Flood of 1864*, 2013, YouTube

Sheffield Libraries Archives & Information, *Sources for the Study of The Sheffield Flood 1864*, 2009-2015

www.sheffieldfloodclaimsarchive.shu.ac.uk

Image Credits

www.picturesheffield.com

Page 3	Sheffield Flood, Dale Dyke Reservoir outside views after bursting , s00973
Page 13	Flood damage at Rowell Bridge Wheel, photographer L Peacock, w00404
Page 15	Remains of F Shaw and Co, wire drawers, Damflask Wire Mill, River Loxley, looking downstream, photographer L Peacock, w00397
Page 19	Coloured engraving of the scene following the Sheffield Flood: Barker and Johnson's crinoline factory, Malin Bridge, Martin Billing, Son and Co, engraver, Birmingham, arc00187
Page 22	The remains of Hill Bridge and Freemasons Arms, Walkley Lane, s10951
Page 24	The remains of Brick Row, Holme Lane, Hillsborough, y00936
Page 27	Memorial card for John Cowton Appleby and his family, s45096
Page 28	Coloured engraving of the scene following the Sheffield Flood, remains of the bridge, Hillsborough, arc00188
Page 55	The remains of the Turner Wheel, Malin Bridge, Hillsborough, w00438
Page 62	John Gunson, engineer, Sheffield Water Company, 1880, s09068

Geoffrey Amey, *The Collapse of the Dale Dyke Dam, 1864,* Cassell & Co., 1974, and Octopus Publishing Group

Pages 9, 10, 11	Maps of the route of the Sheffield Flood

Samuel Harrison, *A Complete History of the Great Flood at Sheffield,* 1898

Page 17	Ruins of Wisewood Works
Page 17	Where the bridge crossed the river at Malin Bridge
Page 26	The ruins at Hillsbro'
Page 31	Mr Hawksley's Mill at Owlerton
Page 31	The Low bridge at Owlerton
Page 43	View from the Ball St Bridge, Sheffield

Malcolm Nunn, Bradfield Archives

Cover image	Photograph taken by Laurence Peacock, near to the Turner Wheel at Malin Bridge

Utmost efforts have been made to ensure copyright compliance.

SHEFFIELD GENERAL CEMETERY

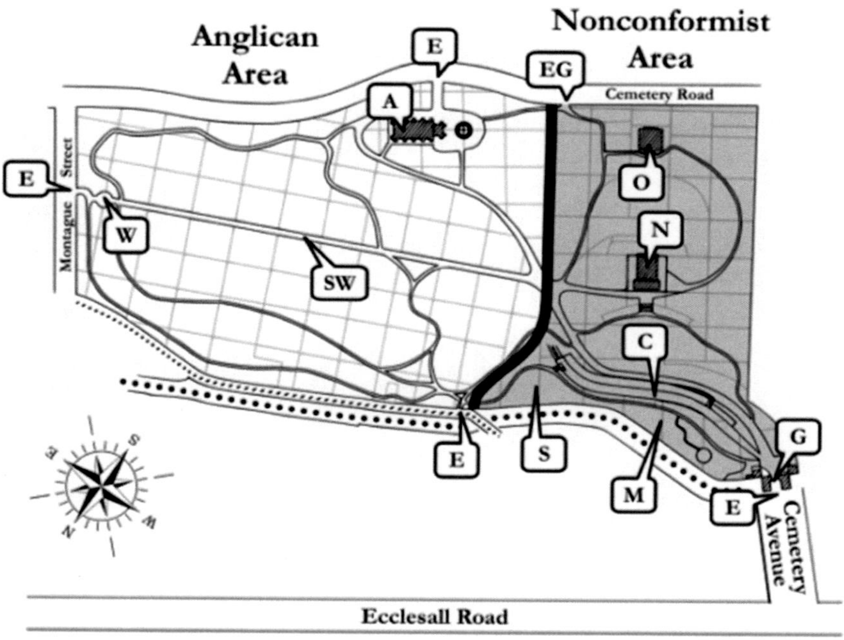

▬	Dissenters' Wall	//////	Stalker Walk
A	Anglican Chapel	•••••	Porter Brook
N	Nonconformist Chapel (Samuel Worth Chapel)	E	Entrance
G	Gatehouse	EG	Egyptian Gate
O	Old Cemetery Office	W	War Memorial
SW	Sandford's Walk	S	Stone Spiral
C	Catacombs	M	Memorial Garden

Sheffield General Cemetery Trust

First opened in 1836, the Cemetery was the final resting place for nearly 86,500 people before closing for burials in 1978.

The Cemetery, now a Listed Grade II* Historic Landscape, lay abandoned and overgrown for many years but has been carefully restored by Sheffield City Council and the Sheffield General Cemetery Trust. The many fine buildings, Victorian monuments and headstones now sit in a delightful parkland landscape of wildflowers and shady trees. The Cemetery Park is a recognised Local Nature Reserve, and its winding paths lead you past some of Sheffield's famous residents, from steel barons to radical chartists.

The Sheffield General Cemetery Trust is a charitable trust which with its committed volunteers maintains and develops the historic landscape and researches the history of the site and people buried there. For over 30 years the Trust has organised events and led tours of the site for the public, schools and community groups. The Trust restored some of its buildings, and the beautiful Samuel Worth Chapel is now available for event hire and the Sexton's Lodge can be hired as overnight accommodation.

Visit our website **www.gencem.org** to find out more about the Cemetery.

Drowned Voices is one of a series of books created by volunteers of the Sheffield General Cemetery Trust which can be purchased through our website at www.gencem.org

Canvas of Memories

Read the stories of the artists who contributed to the growth of Sheffield. They were inspired by the town and its surrounding countryside to produce art which is still inspiring us today. **Price £8.99**

A Woman's Place

Fascinating stories of Sheffield's Victorian women, some of whom fell prey to the perils of widowhood, disease, childbirth and alcoholism, but there were also those who paved the way for the opportunities we enjoy today.

Price £7.99

Sweet Remembrance

The hidden and often secret stories behind graves in the General Cemetery give a fascinating insight into our confectionery past. This book tells many of those stories and explains how they relate to the development of the UK confectionery industry. **Price £17.99**

A Window into the Workhouse

Just over ten percent of all the burials in Sheffield General Cemetery are of people whose last residence was recorded as a workhouse. This book uncovers some of their lives, and the circumstances which led to their admission to the workhouse. **Price £8.99**